Victory and Dominion Over Fear

by
Lester Sumrall, D.Lit., D.D.

Sumrall Publishing Company
South Bend, Indiana

VICTORY & DOMINION OVER FEAR

Printed in the United State of America
All Scripture quotations are from the *King James
Version of the Bible.*

ISBN 0-89274-233-X

Contents

Preface

The primary purpose of every author producing a prose volume should be to meet an immediate need in the hearts and lives of a large segment of society.

This book will challenge one of the greatest evils of our time and assist many suffering persons in becoming conquerors over life-defeating obstacles.

The background material for this book was born in the test tubes of practical and experimental laboratories of human behavior over a period of more than fifty years.

Having lived among peoples of different cultures, I have observed mental illness in many lands. After counseling people in over 100 countries, I have concluded that one of the strangest and most tormenting enemies of man—whether he be black, yellow, or white; cultured or primitive—is *fear*.

The Global March

Fear is on a global march! The outbreak of World War I in 1914 caused the beginning of a great march of fear across the world. The economic depression of the 1930s further accelerated this vicious enemy's march. Material insecurity brought near panic to millions of hearts.

World War II produced more fear. The world advanced from the primitive warfare used at the end of World War I—dropping small bombs from aircraft—to the atomic blasts of Nagasaki and Hiroshima at the end of World War II. All intelligent humans then realized there was no place to hide.

Since World War II, scientists and statesmen have continually predicted the impending extermination of the human race. From this fear, the United Nations was born.

Tensions, caused by devastating fear, grip the hearts of millions of frustrated people. The world is now looking for a political genius who, by bringing peace to the fearful nations, can relieve these tensions.

This book, a positive approach to the subject, contains the answer to your personal fear problems.

FOREWORD

Victory & Dominion Over Fear challenges one of the great haunting evils of mankind—fear. Throughout history, man has struggled with living in a world filled with poverty, disease and war.

This classic book was originally authored by my father, Dr. Lester Sumrall, to help people everywhere deal with the forces of darkness and learn to live victorious lives.

Dad often said, "No matter what the race or culture, fear is one of the most tormenting enemies of man." Certainly in todays believers are often tossed back and forth on the waves of life. As you listen or watch the daily news you are bombarded with fearful images of the Y2K problem, scandals, global warming, contaminated food and water, corporate downswing, the coming social security shortfall, child abuse, divorce, drug abuse murder, war in the Balkans. It is all pretty sobering ... and frightening.

So how are Christians to live in a world filled with so much uncertainty and hopelessness?

The answer is we are not to live in this world. As Christians, we are to live above our circumstances. We know God did not give us a spirit of fear, but a spirit of power, love, and self-control. We also know we are called to serve others and lead the lost to Jesus Christ. As I reflect upon the book of Esther, I see many lessons of believers today. As you recall, Esther was God's woman. placed in a unique position of authority to save the Jewish people from destruction. God put her in the right place at the right time, *"for such a time as this."* Our Lord had dominion over her time just as He has a guiding hand on each of His servants today.

There is no place for fear in the life of the believer. He has placed us where he wants us now, "for such a time as this." We must keep our eyes on Him and where He is leading us. We must never lose sight of our mission as believers to bring others to Christ.

I pray this special edition will bless and strengthen you and your walk with the Lord. I pray too that you will overcome anything in your life that may be holding you back from where The Lord wants to take you and use you.

Yours for the Untold Billions Yet Untold,
Pete Sumrall
April, 1999

1

Unmasking Man's Deadliest Enemy

There is no fear in love; but perfect love casteth out fear: because fear hath torment.
1 John 4:18

Fear has been called the Black Monster. Today this monster is striking with a demonic fury, waging aggressive warfare upon helpless people of all nations. Because of this wicked ogre, multitudes of modern lives are suffering material destruction, moral degradation, and spiritual annihilation.

The Black Monster, which torments rational people, is not the ordinary excitement one feels after hearing a sudden noise or when performing a perilous task. This monster, unmasked, is an unreasoning, tormenting, persisting fear that makes life difficult and distressing, blacking out people's personalities with dark clouds of apprehension and hallucination.

Universal Fear

The problem most often presented to me by people of every color and social position throughout the world is the problem of fear.

In addition to religious leaders, thinking people from all other walks of life are alert to this onslaught of fear. Herbert Hoover, a former president of the United States, summarized what he learned during an official world tour upon his return to America: "The dominant emotion everywhere in the world is *fear*. This applies to every part of human activities—finance, industry, farmers, workers, thinkers, and government officials.'' This painful and heart-stirring report is from a wise statesman and qualified observer.

Medical authorities also realize that the world is in the iron-clasped grip of an invisible enemy, whose unrelenting stranglehold is destroying the vital life of society. Doctors fight an increasing number of battles against this real, yet unreal, monster in their patients. They are studying more and more the mental man along with the physical man.

In the political arena, world rulers are almost to the same frustration point that King Belshazzar reached. The night his empire dissolved into the rubble of history amid the wine, women, and song of a state banquet, the Bible says, *The king's countenance was changed . . . the joints of his loins were loosed, and his knees smote one against another* (Dan. 5:6).

The cause of fear in that day was the organized might of the victorious Medes and Persians. Today it is the awful blasts of atomic bombs, intercontinental missiles, germ warfare, and deadly rays from outer space. Statesmen are among those most aware that there is no place to hide.

The Atlantic Charter

In his first inaugural speech, the late Franklin Delano Roosevelt, president of the United States and skillful statesman, said: "So first of all, let me assert my firm belief that the only thing we have to fear is fear itself—nameless, unreasoning, unjustified terror."

At a secret rendezvous in the Atlantic Ocean, President Roosevelt and British Prime Minister Winston Churchill drew up the historic document known as the Atlantic Charter. This modern "Magna Carta" is considered one of the greatest charters championing the common liberties of mankind. It will be remembered throughout history for its Four

Freedoms: Freedom from Want, Freedom from Fear, Freedom of Speech, and Freedom of Religion.

During the most dreadful conflict of history, these statesmen listed fear as one of the four major evils of the world. Our modern world is enslaved by fear of war, secret police, hunger, and oppression. These Allied statesmen solemnly vowed to give themselves to the fight against the Black Monster of fear.

Every rational person should devote himself to fighting this vicious monster. Some of the greatest human tragedies have befallen those who are victims of fear. Without doubt, fear is the deadliest enemy of all people.

Who and Why

Fear respects no one. It haunts the unlearned and the university educated alike. It strikes at the highborn and those of humble origin. It walks the floors of the mansion and palace as well as the floors of the hut. Men from all walks of life have failed equally in the entrusted job of building a successful and happy life—a job which prepares one to live forever with God.

Unmasking the Monster

The hideous Black Monster must be unmasked. To do so, we cannot deal with it collectively. For personal results, we must disclose fear's effects on individuals.

Real Fear and Shadow Fear

The first step toward deliverance from this diabolical monster is to know that two kinds of fear exist: *real fear* and *shadow fear*. You would feel *real fear* if you were to meet an uncaged lion! If you fear something that does not exist, you are experiencing *shadow* fear. Maladjusted personalities result from *shadow* fear. This unreal fear is what we must fight.

Positive and Negative Fears

One of the newer translations of the Bible describes both a positive fear and a negative one. Fear can be either a profitable servant, or an overbearing master!

Positive fear can be described as reverence and respect. The Bible says we are to fear God, but this fear is unrelated to horror or terror. It is the same "fear" a child has for his parents.

When I was a boy, my father would delegate some small duty for me to perform during his absence. If I performed that duty well, I waited at the front gate for his approval and reward. But if I had failed to do my duty, I made myself difficult to find! I was afraid to meet my father.

The Christian loves God and "waits at the gate" for His approval, but the sinner does not want to see God; he is afraid of God. The type of fear, positive or negative, that one feels depends upon whether or not he has done his duty.

Facing Fears

When a person "feels afraid," what does he feel?

It is impossible to feel thought, but you can feel physical changes caused by a thought: your heart pounding out of control, your stomach churning like an angry sea, your legs trembling like an aspen leaf in a March wind.

Neurologists teach that the lower central part of the brain, the *thalamus* is the center of emotions. From the thalamus, thoughts of fear propel their impulses, manufacturing imaginary worries and fear phobias.

Also in this nerve center, affection and love are born; therefore, *He that ruleth his spirit* (is better) *than he that taketh a city* (Prov. 16:32). This knowledge is important because it reveals that if a person dispatches the proper messages from his thalamus, he will win the battle of life!

Imagination and Fear

This information reveals further that tormenting fears are not based upon anything real. They are unfounded conditions and emotions from within, not without.

One New York City doctor has said that humans are born with two normal fears: fear of sudden noise or sound, and fear of unexpected withdrawal of support. All other fears are a result of mental confusion and must be learned.

A notable truth is that rational persons are born with confidence. Babies are unaware that they have enemies. They must be taught whom to trust and whom not to trust.

Fellow rational human beings teach infants that they are surrounded by enemies, powerful and persistent ones. They teach them that to live resourcefully, humans must know how to conquer these enemies and how to trust friends who are waging battle with common enemies. Unfortunately, many of these enemies are imaginary. Yet, they harm the personality as if they were real.

Fears Become Phobias

Looking through a house of broken personalities is indeed sad. One observes all degrees of ill health: from those who have lapsed temporarily from normalcy to those who are classified as incurable by human standards. In many instances, these persons permitted their petty fears to become powerful phobias. When a person consistently reacts unreasonably to a fear, he has permitted it to become a phobia.

Here is a list of modern phobias which plague humanity:

agoraphobia	fear of open spaces, of going where people are
ailurophobia	fear of cats
algophobia	fear of pain
androphobia	fear of men
anemophobia	fear of winds or drafts
aphephobia	aversion to being touched
arachnephobia	fear of spiders
astrephobia	fear of thunderstorms
astrophobia	fear of the sky
autophobia	fear of being alone
basiphobia	fear of walking
bathophobia	fear of falling from high places
batophobia	fear of high objects (towers, mountains)
carophobia	fear of insects
coprophobia	repugnance to filth, dirt
cynophobia	fear of dogs, of getting rabies
demophobia	fear of crowds
doraphobia	fear of touching animal hair or fur
ergasiophobia	dislike of work, fear of taking responsibility

gamophobia	fear of marriage
gehrophobia	fear of crossing bridge over water
gynephobia	fear of women
hemophobia	fear of sight of blood
lalophobia	fear of public speaking
lyssophobia	fear of going insane
misophobia	fear of hatred
necrophobia	fear of dead bodies
nudophobia	fear of being seen unclothed
ophidiophobia	fear of snakes
pantophobia	fear of the future
peccatophobia	fear of committing social errors or sinning
pharmacophobia	fear of medicine
psychrophobia	fear of cold
pyrophobia	fear of fire
rhabdophobia	fear of being beaten
scopophobia	fear of being observed
scotophobia	fear of darkness
sitophobia	fear of eating
thalassaphobia	fear of sea voyage
toxicophobia	fear of being poisoned
zoophobia	fear of animals in general

2

The Origin of Fear

I heard thy voice in the garden, and I was afraid . . . and I hid myself.

Genesis 3:10

Researching for a solution to a problem is unsuccessful until the true source of the problem is discovered. One must know a problem's cause before attempting to remedy its effects. In seeking a solution to the ravaging effects of fear, one must first know its cause. Human fear cannot be eliminated until a rational and spiritual study of its origin is completed.

When those cursed with poisonous fear phobias understand the history of the Black Monster of fear, their victory will be half won! They will possess courage to fight back!

The story of fear's origin takes us back to the dawn of human history, beginning in the Garden of Eden, the paradise which God created for man. After beautifying it with every gorgeous flower and stocking it with plumaged birds and strong roving beasts, God appointed man to be the sovereign ruler over this exotic utopia.

God gave man dominion over this great domain, the entire earth-world, with all its material wealth and wonderful creatures. (Gen. 1:27,28.) Fear was unknown in the bliss and beauty of this Garden of God. Man was completely unafraid!

The Birth of Fear

How did the cloud of fear first settle over man's mind and soul? If man was created to have dominion, how could cowardly fear conquer him?

On the day that Adam, the legal head of the human race, willfully and rebelliously broke the law and trust of God, man's heart became an incubator for fear, frustration, uncertainty, and foreboding.

The first rational transgression birthed human fear. For the first time, cowardice was in man's heart. He hid himself among the trees because he was afraid. (Gen. 3:8.) On that awful day with all its ugly and demoralizing effects upon the human personality, fear was born.

The fall of man in Eden's Garden became the source of all human fear. Sin and transgression is the father of fear. The Devil, who tempted Adam and Eve to rebel against God, is fear's originator. No wonder God's Word states that the devils believe and tremble. (James 2:19.) The original sins that the demons committed before the dawn of history damned them and created fear in them. All demons know their day of judgment is near. (Matt. 8:29.)

The Growth of Fear

Who are the primary producers of the evil Black Monster in this twentieth century? There are several.

Satan

Satan—the Devil, the Evil One—is public enemy number one in producing fear. Fear is his strongest instrument or weapon for breaking the personality of man and destroying his life.

By using fear Satan separates man from his Maker. When in fear, man cannot have faith. I have found that in those countries where Satan has the largest following, fear is most widespread. The heathen live in constant fear. Almost all of their religious activities are performed to pacify the wrath of their pagan deities.

J. W. Westgarth, author of *The Holy Spirit and the Primitive Mind*, says: "Inborn fear, characteristic of the African, believes that insidious subterranean forces are at work against him . . . he keeps medicine on his body, in boxes in his home, or buried nearby to protect himself" (p. 42). Only the Devil could make a human so afraid.

An African explained his fears to missionary Westgarth: "Sin made me a coward. When I was walking through the bush paths at night, I was always afraid and hurried home, but even then I felt no security. Since I set matters right with God, I have had no fear . . ." (p. 45).

Evil Spirits

In addition to Satan, evil spirits (called demons in the Bible), ruled by Satan, labor incessantly to bring fear into the lives of humans.

The example given in Matthew 8:32 is typical in biblical history of demons' fear-raising operations. This verse describes a herd of swine which ran violently into the sea to perish after demons possessed them. The Bible relates several accounts of demons inflicting pain and terror upon humans.

Dominating Humans

Some wicked men and women take a special delight in making others fearful. A big bully of a man wants all his acquaintances to fear him. He frightens the weak and helpless with the proud, boastful words he speaks about his courage and strength.

Unwise Parents

There are unwise parents who actually seem to take delight in making their small children afraid of them. They curse them loudly, beat them brutally, and threaten them continually.

Advertisers

Advertisers often use fear strategy sales techniques such as, "Use Brand-X to avoid halitosis," or "Watch out for B.O.—your friends do!"

Some insurance salesmen play on fear to sell their policies. They use funeral-toned words that create images of impending doom, centered around poor starving orphans and widows. I believe that as good stewards of God we should not be swayed by these techniques, but should always spend money intelligently.

Religion

Religion, I am sad to admit, is one of the greatest agencies for producing fear. Some religions thrive on fear-dominated disciples. Their entire theology is built upon fearful deities with avenging hatreds. Often when the truth is presented to them, they will say, "My religion will not permit me to listen!'' I have actually heard them say, ''I know my religion is wrong, but I'm afraid to leave it because of what I would suffer.''

Now that we know the origin of the Black Monster and are aware of its primary producers, we are ready to study the effects of fear on man's personality. Then we will learn how to get victory and dominion over fear.

3

How Fear Attacks

And he answering said, Thou shalt love the Lord thy God with all thy heart, and with all thy soul, and with all thy strength, and with all thy mind; and thy neighbour as thyself.

Luke 10:27

The Physical Attack

Millions of people live in anguish, fearing terrible diseases. Thousands of adults, fearing cancer, diagnose every stomach pain or pimple on the skin as the beginning of that disease. Prompted by anxiety, families spend millions of dollars to prevent receiving diseases which, more than likely, they will never have.

The tissue and organs of our bodies can be affected by these negative emotions. Fear, a mental action, takes its toll, producing actual physical illness and disease.

The following words from the ancient book of Job reveal God's wisdom:

For the thing which I greatly feared is come upon me, and that which I was afraid of is come unto me.

Job 3:25

Fear and the Corporal Body

Modern therapeutic science has discovered that fear can cause stomach ulcers, insomnia, nervous breakdowns, mental depressions, throat colds, head disorders, and also contributes to hypertension (high blood pressure) which leads each day to the deaths of a thousand Americans and tens of thousands of humans around the world.

Outstanding medical authorities acknowledge the proven evils of fear. A physician at famous St. Bartholomew's Hospital in London, England, showed that fifty percent of all people suffering from acute heart ailments fell ill after some excitement caused by social, family, or economic worries. The renowned American physician, Dr. Alexis S. Carroll, states: "Fear is capable of starting a genuine disease."

This is revolutionary thinking in modern medical circles. Once doctors used drugs and surgery only, but in this age of tensions and hyper-tensions, doctors acknowledge a need for another kind of treatment. They see an illness that goes back to the human soul. In analyzing this type of illness, S. H. Kraines and E. S. Thetford, coauthors of the book, *Managing Your Mind*, concluded, "Fear contributes to physical illness."

A woman recently said to her doctor: "I am full of fear; I can't go out by myself. I feel so mixed up and dizzy and weak. I haven't had a decent night's sleep in months. My mind is in a whirl. I'm frightened! I know something dreadful is going to happen to me!"

This is the sad testimony of many helpless people today. An acquaintance told me that fear of losing his job caused him to have chronic nausea and stomach cramps.

Medical experts find that children who don't like their studies or teacher, or who fear school in general, can develop a "Monday to Friday" eczema, which miraculously improves over the weekend.

Beyond contradiction, fear has caused our bodies to become targets of the Devil. God has ordained that our bodies be the temples of the Holy Spirit; therefore, they must not be fear ridden.

Medication cannot heal fear sickness. Christ, the Great Physician, has the exact prescription. Anyone willing to receive may have it free for the asking.

The Mental Attack

Fear strikes at the stronghold of the human mind—the central government of the human personality.

Being ill in the mind is far more critical than being ill in any other way. For this reason, the Devil makes the man's mind the central place of warfare. He knows that if he conquers the mind, man has no chance of having a normal life.

Supernatural fear affecting the mind can ruin the nervous system. It can spoil an otherwise pleasing personality.

Mental Evils

Fear gives birth to many mental evils. Explanations of several follow:

1. Chronic Melancholia

R. Howard, M.D., of England states: "In the whole realm of medicine, there is nothing so terrible to contemplate as a man with chronic melancholia." (*Problem of Pain*, by C. S. Lewis)

Melancholia is an unreasoning and unreasonable pessimism. It is expecting the worst, allowing evil to outweigh the good. Its victims call white black and sweet bitter. They are convinced that they are right and everyone else is wrong. Doctors would rather work with a contagious disease than to try pulling someone out of the depths of melancholia.

Having counseled several such persons in this way, I know it to be a slow process. I begin by leading the person in a search through his memories for causes of sadness, depression, and disappointment. Then I carefully show him that instead of reacting negatively to each incident, he can look at each case in another way, a positive way. The final and most important step comes after gaining the person's complete confidence: I pray a sincere prayer of deliverance. This will break the Devil's power and turn on the sunshine of God in that person's mind.

2. Worry

One noted psychiatrist says that worry is a form of fear. This reveals how fear thrives in the dark corners and deep crevices of the mind, creating mental festers. Worry puts wrinkles in the brow, silver in the hair, and passion in the bloodstream. It thwarts our dreams of happiness and success.

Millions of people worry. Some can give logical reasons for worrying, but others have no idea why they are worrying.

I read recently that when Philip D. Armour, the packing house magnate, was a young man establishing himself in business, he fell heavily into debt. One day his banker called on him and said, "I'm worried about your loan at our bank."

"Well," the young man replied, "no use in both of us worrying about the same thing!"

I don't know how far that banker got in life, but I do know one thing: Most of the modern world knows about Armour's hams! Mr. Armour had found that the secret of refusing worry is to take a positive action.

There is the story of a Methodist bishop who was sitting at his desk in his parish one night, worrying about the state of church affairs. He was very troubled, questioning which course to take until the big clock struck twelve. At midnight he heard the voice of the Lord say, "Now, go to bed, Bishop; I will sit up the rest of the night!"

Worry very simply is useless and worthless, and usually worsens a situation.

3. Fear of Condemnation

A haunting fear that tracks many men and women like a demon bloodhound is fear of condemnation. It makes you jump, even though you are guilty of no wrong. You jump when you meet an authority figure such as your employer or when you see a policeman.

The Bible says, *There is therefore now no condemnation to them which are in Christ Jesus* (Rom. 8:1).

A born-again person should never have a self-incriminating conscience. He should not fear the past because it is covered by the blood of Jesus. He should not fear the present because Christ dwells within. He should not fear the future for Christ has promised never to leave us nor forsake us. (Heb. 13:5.)

The inner world of thought should be covered by the protecting power of the blood of Christ and under the direct control of the Holy Spirit. The Holy Spirit can bring into captivity *every* thought to the obedience of Christ. Paul said, . . . *and be renewed in the spirit of your mind* (Eph. 4:23). The word *renewed* means to make over! Our old minds are made new by Christ's divine power. His mental life entering our mental life will remove the old and bring in the new.

A Christian should enter into a covenant with God concerning his mind, just as definitely as he does concerning his soul for salvation, or his body for healing. When he does, the new man—the new creation—will also possess a new mind, and he will no longer live under constant condemnation.

The Christian's Mind

Christians need never spend a night of worrying, then rise from their beds mentally beaten, physically whipped, and unable to do their daily work. Christ has provided rest for the minds of His disciples. Sweet sleep is promised in God's Word: *When thou liest down, thou shalt not be afraid: yea, thou shalt lie down, and thy sleep shall be sweet* (Prov. 3:24).

In my ministry to the nations, I have met many victims of satanic mental attacks upon their personalities. The following are descriptions of several of these cases. Through these examples, one can see how a person can be delivered by the authority of the Lord Jesus Christ.

The Man in Japan

Several years ago while ministering together in Japan, Rev. Howard Carter and I were urged to visit a missionary who was suffering from a strange malady. This man, formerly a successful missionary, had for many months refused to leave his home, saying that he knew the police were looking for him. Fearing that someone would see into his house, he kept the drapes drawn. He never shaved for fear that he would cut himself and die.

Needless to say, his mental life was a wreck, and his patient wife was suffering untold agonies from doing all she knew how to do to assist him.

Rev. Carter and I talked at length with the man and sympathetically listened to his story. Then we read God's Word to him and knelt in prayer.

After we had prayed, I said, "Now we must act." I asked his wife for a pair of scissors and a safety razor. I told the man that since Christ had now delivered him, he must have a shave. I clipped off several months' growth of beard with the scissors, then lathered his face for a shave. Sure enough, when I had finished, he liked what he saw in the mirror.

Then we told him that the three of us were going for a walk and that we would keep him between us to protect him. As we walked, he saw that no police were watching for him. Slowly, he realized that his fears had been imaginary and returned to his home a happy man.

God healed that man's mind. Soon after that, he and his wife took a furlough to their home country. When I last heard from him, he was a normal and happy man in his newfound freedom.

The Woman in South Bend

In South Bend, Indiana, a devoted Christian, who attended my church, became afraid to remain in her lovely home while her husband was at work. The moment he walked out the door, fear struck. The four walls around her terrified her. She often ran from her home to seek refuge in the homes of her neighbors and friends. She remained away until her husband returned from work in the evening.

The Black Monster of fear caused constant confusion in this home. The husband could not understand her, and she could not understand her fear.

She told me her story and requested prayer. I asked if she would completely obey my suggestions. She promised that she would. In obedience to the Bible, I laid hands on her head in the name of the Lord Jesus and commanded the spirit of fear to come out of her and not return. As she was not in pain, I did not expect her to feel too differently. However, she said something like a cloud had lifted from her.

These were my instructions to her:

"Tomorrow morning when your husband starts to leave for work, accompany him to the front door. Do not permit him to close the door; close it yourself.

"Step into the middle of the room and speak these words, 'I resist every power of the Devil. I plead for the blood of Jesus to cover my life and home.' Then start singing a church hymn and begin your household duties."

It worked. Prayer and positive believing delivered that woman from fear and restored her home to its former tranquility.

The Youth in England

In London, England, a Christian young man approached me and confided that he was shackled with agoraphobia—a fear of open places. He said that if he walked across an open field or a city park, his nerves went jittery and his stomach became nauseated. Many times some inward force compelled him to run, panting for breath, to some closed place.

I gave the young man some scriptures for deliverance by God's power. I asked him if he believed them. When he replied in the affirmative, I prayed over him, rebuking the unreasonable power of fear. A letter from him two weeks later described his new lease on life. God had taken fear from his heart! He was completely at ease when walking through parks or woodlands.

The Old Woman in Chicago

Paranoia is a medical term for a delusion of unmerited persecution. In Chicago a few years ago, I was preaching for the Christian Business Men's noon-hour radio broadcast. After the service, a poor, decrepit-looking old lady, whom I had already been observing for several days, slipped up close to me and whispered excitedly: "Sir, all these people here are against me."

I leaned over toward her and whispered back, "Who is against you?"

Pointing to the leader of the meeting, a businessman and Christian gentleman, she said, "He is one!"

Then I inquired sympathetically: "Anybody else?"

She raised her bony finger, pointed to a number of businessmen, and whispered, "All these people are against me!"

Had I not seen the terror on her wrinkled face, I would have laughed. She was firmly convinced that those professional Christian men of Chicago, occupied with weighty burdens of business and God's work, were against her, though they did not even know her.

Laying a hand on her shoulder, I promised to help, instructing her that she must not worry anymore.

She nodded her head approvingly and whispered, "Thank you, sir." Then she walked away. I watched as she stopped at the door of the building and looked in all directions to be sure that none of her "enemies" would see or follow her before moving out quickly.

To any normal person, that old lady's actions would seem silly, yet her life was miserable because of this devilish monster of fear. Divine deliverance was her only hope.

The Man in Manila

In Manila, Philippines, a Chinese businessman came to see me. When I stretched out my hand to greet him, he pulled his hands back saying, "I cannot shake your hand; you may have a contagious disease." He shook hands with no one. He said that he felt contaminated by everything he touched and washed his hands from fifty to a hundred times a day. His hands were powdered white as snow with a special disinfectant.

This man, a pitiful sight to behold, was tormented by coprophobia—a fear of dirt. He came to me for prayer, but he did not want me to touch his body in doing so. He did not permit even members of his family to touch him. He spent his days and nights washing away that which did not exist.

He was one who had not met and recognized his fears. Having withdrawn himself from actuality, he had lost touch with vibrant, exciting, and joyful life. He existed on delusions, misconceptions, and imaginations, failing spiritually and emotionally to distinguish between the real and the unreal—the absolute basis for all happiness.

There Is an Answer

One could describe endlessly these unfortunate souls who are victims of the Devil's tormenting game of nerves. They are rational people suffering deep agony from irrational fear. They are disturbed souls living in an earthly hell, bound by invisible, but powerful, chains.

Are *you* suffering from a continual lack of peace, from nagging anxiety or constant confusion? Is there fear in *your* mind, heart, and soul? Do *you* fear society or meeting people? Are *you* afraid of losing your job? Do *you* fear going insane?

If so, you can have deliverance. A loving God, Who does not want you to be tormented by fear, will deliver you.

The Spiritual Attack

Fear can influence the spirit and soul of man. Persistent fears cause spiritual paralysis. No man who has a heart of fear is capable of great feats of spiritual attainment.

Fear is a chain that binds the soul, a force that breaks communion with God. A fearful person cannot live in the presence of God.

The truly great men of history were men who overcame fear. The roots of their faith went deep into the sacred love of the Creator of the universe. They knew Him; and because they knew Him, they did not *fear*. Chapter 11 of Hebrews describes some of these heroes of faith.

To Abraham, God said: "Fear not!" Abraham believed and became one of the greatest men of all history.

Moses was not afraid. Though it meant incurring the wrath of the emperor, he refused to be called the son of Pharaoh's daughter. He led forth from Egypt some three million slaves who became the great nation of Israel.

Joshua was not afraid. Even though warring kings and soldiers outnumbered him, they crumbled before his daring faith.

David was not afraid. He could fight a bear, a lion, a giant. He said, *Though I walk through the valley of the shadow of death, I will fear no evil: for thou art with me* . . . (Ps. 23:4).

Fear brings spiritual poverty to the soul. The gifts and fruits of the Spirit wither and die under the continued successful assault of fear.

For a healthy spiritual life, Christians must live above fear. A commanding and outstanding difference between the believer and the unbeliever must exist.

Greater is he that is in you, than he that is in the world.

1 John 4:4

4
Fear and the End of the World

. . . Men's hearts failing them for fear, and for looking after those things which are coming on the earth . . .

Luke 21:26

Never before in history has society known the tremendous number of broken mental personalities as exist in this generation. The number of people seeking medical treatment for "nerves and emotional tensions" is greater today than the total of people suffering from all other sicknesses combined.

When men and women of modern society should have less to worry about, they are setting an all-time record for worry and frustration! There *is* a cause! The reason for this tremendous increase in fear phobias throughout the world must be stated and proven. Disclosing the true cause of fear is especially necessary at a time when modern science and education are aggressively attempting to stamp out ignorance and superstition.

The Reason

Fear has a prophetical meaning. Since the first law was broken in the Garden of Eden, human fear has always existed because it is the fruit of disobedience. However, one of the certain end signs of the present world system and the return of the Lord Jesus Christ to the earth, is the many deadly, black, demonlike fears corrupting human society.

Proving from the Bible that the worldwide outbreak of fear is a prophetical sign of the end of the world as we know it, will give us an all-renewed courage to prevent fear from overwhelming us as we battle against it.

Christ Prophesied Fear

We agree that the authority of the Lord Jesus Christ as a world redeemer stands or falls by the accuracy of His predictions. He is either a true prophet or a false prophet—there can be no neutral ground.

Evidence throughout history, including current events, establishes Jesus of Nazareth as a true prophet of the Living God. His predictions have become a blueprint of history. Christians can stake their eternal lives upon the truth of His prophecies.

The beloved physician, Luke, recorded a great prophecy spoken by Christ about the end of time. The Lord said:

And there shall be signs in the sun, and in the moon, and in the stars; and upon the earth distress of nations, with perplexity; the sea and the waves roaring;

Men's hearts failing them for fear, and for looking after those things which are coming on the earth: for the powers of heaven shall be shaken.

And then shall they see the Son of man coming in a cloud with power and great glory.

And when these things begin to come to pass, then look up, and lift up your heads; for your redemption draweth nigh.

Luke 21:25-28

Here Christ predicted cosmic disturbances in the heavens as an end-time sign. Since the time of Noah and the Flood, there have been cosmic disturbances. According to historical records, these disturbances have greatly accelerated within the last century.

The entire news media—daily newspapers, magazines, radio, and television—inform us of the horrible disasters of earthquakes in many lands. They tell of tidal waves, typhoons, hurricanes, and cyclones occurring in our present day.

Having been caught in a typhoon myself, I know its power. Its winds roared up to 125 miles per hour, uprooting trees, destroying houses, killing and wounding many. Words cannot describe the feeling as the building you are in sways back and forth under a wind so powerful that it sounds like thunder.

Christ prophesied, *There shall be . . . upon the earth distress of nations, with perplexity.* Could anyone describe present world conditions with better words? Yet Christ spoke these words almost 2000 years ago. He meant them as a sign to alert those living near the time of His return and the end of the world.

Jesus also declared that men's hearts would be *failing them for fear, and for looking after those things which are coming on the earth.*

Christ plainly predicted today's fear phobias: that men and women observing civilization's present-day circumstances would find their hearts gripped by deadly fear.

The great number of suicides among well-known industrialists in many countries today is evidence of this dreadful fear mania. Their hearts could not stand the pressure of what they could see coming upon this world.

Political leaders have suffered in a similar way. As they have observed the horizons black with national and international strife and bloodshed, their hearts have melted. And the layman, without a technical knowledge of coming events, feels the very air filled with fear.

As the horrible holocaust of Armageddon slowly draws nearer, this sinful and rebellious world becomes more and more fearful.

Isaiah's Prophecy

In addition to the great prophecies of Christ regarding fear in the last days, the Bible also records descriptions given by Old and New Testament prophets of the condition of men's hearts at the end of the age.

Isaiah, the greatest prophet of the Old Testament, saw the end of time and prophesied of these conditions:

For the day of the Lord of hosts shall be upon every one that is proud and lofty, and upon every one that is lifted up; and he shall be brought low . . .

And they shall go into the holes of the rocks, and into the caves of the earth, for fear of the Lord, and for the glory of his majesty, when he ariseth to shake terribly the earth.

In that day a man shall cast his idols of silver, and his idols of gold, which they made each one for himself to worship, to the moles and to the bats;

To go into the clefts of the rocks, and into the tops of the ragged rocks, for fear of the Lord, and for the glory of his majesty, when he ariseth to shake terribly the earth.

Cease ye from man, whose breath is in his nostrils: for wherein is he to be accounted of?

Isaiah 2:12,19-22

All students of prophecy identify the "day of the Lord of hosts" with the end of Gentile rule in world affairs. At that terrible time the proud sinners of the world, in trying to hide themselves from a righteous God, shall seek refuge in rocks and mountain hideouts.

Today nations are ready to make their abode and hiding place in the holes and rocks of the earth. This condition brings an intense fear into the hearts of mankind.

Solomon Says . . .

When man has run God's last red light and finds himself abandoned of a Savior, even his prayers will profit nothing.

Solomon, the wise seer of Israel, wrote these words:

I also will laugh at your calamity; I will mock when your fear cometh;

When your fear cometh as desolation, and your destruction cometh as a whirlwind; when distress and anguish cometh upon you.

Then shall they call upon me, but I will not answer; they shall seek me early, but they shall not find me . . .

But whoso hearkeneth unto me shall dwell safely, and shall be quiet from fear of evil.

Proverbs 1:26-28,33

Solomon with his God-given wisdom saw a time when fear, desolation, distress, and anguish would come upon mankind.

John's Revelation

In the New Testament, John, the Beloved Disciple, predicted in the Revelation that the time would come when men and women would hide in the holes of the earth for fear of the things that were coming to pass. (Rev. 6:15-17.)

He was prophetically previewing modern atomic bombs, germ warfare, and cosmic rays from outer space.

5

The Master's Mind

For who hath known the mind of the Lord, that he may instruct him? But we have the mind of Christ.

1 Corinthians 2:16

In this confusing twentieth century world, many teachers and leaders cannot live up to their own theories and philosophies.

Because of the critical conditions of our times, the leader must lead; the guide must show the way; the doctor must heal himself. Authors of well-known books on the subject of dealing with people should not be having matrimonial problems which end in divorce. Noted psychiatrists should not be suffering from mental delusions and on the verge of nervous collapse.

Examining the Master's Mind

Christians have a perfect right to examine carefully the thinking of Jesus of Nazareth. Christians should be sure that the One they follow lives up to the high standard of His teachings.

The New Testament is a picture book of the mind of Christ. Through it, we can travel with the Master over the rough trails of life. We can follow Him through the dark, musty streets of poverty-ridden, diseased, and fearful people and observe His mental attitudes.

Millions of people seek to understand the doctrines of Christ in order to follow Him spiritually and morally. They should study also His mental habits and attitudes, then seek to be like Him in that way as well.

Since Christ was divine as well as human when He walked among men nearly twenty centuries ago, no man has been able to fathom the depths or measure the heights of the Master's mind. So great a mind had never existed before, and no other has since. But the Holy Spirit will assist us in seeing and following Jesus.

His Mind and Men

The Lord Jesus knew the mind of all men. He was not taught by man how to analyze character, nor did He need to get to know a man in order to understand him. The Master knew the mind of men by spiritual discernment. We see this revealed in the Gospel of Luke:

And the chief priests and the scribes the same hour sought to lay hands on him; and they feared the people: for they perceived that he had spoken this parable against them.

And they watched him, and sent forth spies, which should feign themselves just men, that they might take hold of his words, that so they might deliver him unto the power and authority of the governor.

And they asked him, saying, Master, we know that thou sayest and teachest rightly, neither acceptest thou the person of any, but teachest the way of God truly:

Is it lawful for us to give tribute unto Caesar, or no?

But he perceived their craftiness, and said unto them, Why tempt ye me? Shew me a penny. Whose image and superscription hath it?

They answered and said, Caesar's.

And he said unto them, Render therefore unto Caesar the things which be Caesar's, and unto God the things which be God's.

And they could not take hold of his words before the people: and they marvelled at his answer, and held their peace.

Luke 20:19-26

When Jesus met Peter, He gave him a new name:

And he (Andrew) brought him to Jesus. And when Jesus beheld him, he said, Thou art Simon the son of Jona: Thou shalt be called Cephas, which is by interpretation, A stone.

John 1:42

It took Peter a long time to understand Jesus, but Jesus knew Peter the first moment of their meeting, even giving him a name representative of his nature.

When Philip urged his friend Nathanael to come and observe Christ, Nathanael remarked, *Can there be any good thing come out of Nazareth?* (John 1:46). But after he met Jesus, he changed his thinking.

Jesus saw Nathanael coming to him, and saith of him, Behold an Israelite indeed, in whom is no guile!

Nathanael saith unto him, Whence knowest thou me? Jesus answered and said unto him, Before that Philip called thee, when thou wast under the fig tree, I saw thee (vv. 47,48).

Nathanael had never encountered anyone with such a mind. His experience with Jesus, related in the above passage, proved to him the messiahship of Christ. (John 1:49.)

Christ knew the mind of King Herod. He publicly called him a "fox" because of his unstable political policies. (Luke 13:32.)

His Mind and Peace

No man has ever known peace of mind as did Christ. He spoke with the deepest assurances of His knowledge of God and of His certainty of the future.

Many times He demonstrated clearly His peace of mind in His public life. When the disciples feared that the great storm raging on the Sea of Galilee would capsize their boat and cause all of them to perish, the Lord Jesus calmly and firmly said, *Peace, be still* (Mark 4:39). To the fishermen's amazement, the tempestuous waves ceased instantly. Christ knew no fear of nature.

His Mind and Danger

Christ was afraid of neither men nor devils.

Mark 5:1-13 records the exciting story of the wild man of Gadara who was possessed with 2000 angry, screaming devils. Anyone who had faced those tormenting spirits had trembled with terror. But as the wild man faced the Nazarene and heard His positive, commanding words, *Come out of the man, thou unclean spirit* (v. 8), he felt the peace of heaven come into his heart and mind. The devils were made to obey Christ's powerful words.

Christ was never afraid in any circumstance of danger. When Pilate's armed guards came to capture Him as He was praying in the Garden of Gethsemene, Christ assisted them. In looking for their prisoner, the confused guards, waved their swords and spears, frightening Jesus' disciples. In response to Jesus' question, *Whom seek ye?* the guards snarled, "Jesus of Nazareth!" Jesus, in the kindest and calmest voice, assured them, *I am he* (John 18:4,5).

Christ's mind never knew panic or fear.

His Mind and Death

If a man weakens, it will be at his death. At that moment all hypocrisy pulls aside to reveal the man as he really is. As Christ approached the time of His death, He showed no sign of fear, only pure victory.

We see His courageous mind more clearly at Calvary than at any other time in His life. As the sharp, cruel nails pinned His hands to the rugged cross on Golgotha's hill, His mind remained extremely alert. He uttered these seven historic affirmations:

1. The Affirmation of Propitiation: *Father, forgive them; for they know not what they do* (Luke 23:34).

2. The Affirmation of Pardon: *To day shalt thou be with me in paradise* (Luke 23:43).

3. The Affirmation of Provision: *Woman, behold thy son! . . . Behold thy mother!* (John 19:26,27).

4. The Affirmation of Atonement: *My God, my God, why hast thou forsaken me?* (Mark 15:34).

5. The Affirmation of Expiation: *I thirst* (John 19:28).

6. The Affirmation of Exaltation: *It is finished* (John 19:30).

7. The Affirmation of Expiration: *Father, into thy hands I commend my spirit* (Luke 23:46).

These are words of forgiveness, salvation, affection, suffering, victory—but none are of fear.

The Apostle Paul said, . . . *we have the mind of Christ* (1 Cor. 2:16). May this be the prayer of each of us today.

6
My Personal Victory

Fear thou not; for I am with thee: be not dismayed; for I am thy God: I will strengthen thee; yea, I will help thee; yea, I will uphold thee with the right hand of my righteousness.

Behold, all they that were incensed against thee shall be ashamed and confounded: they shall be as nothing; and they that strive with thee shall perish.
Isaiah 41:10,11

A soldier without battle scars cannot effectively teach others to war. Readers want to know an author's personal experience concerning the subject being covered in his book.

I have faced many fearful situations in my life—the guns of bandits; the knives of killers; the stones of religious fanatics; the strange, unseen powers of evil in demon-infested communities. Several times I have prayed what I thought could be my last prayer. Only by God's grace, am I not a fear victim.

A Youth Meets God

I was not brought through the dark night of fear into the golden sunlight of faith by a kind friend, but only by *God's Holy Word*.

When I was seventeen years of age, God healed my body of tuberculosis in both lungs. (Recent X rays still reveal the scars.) After my healing, God divinely sent me to proclaim His Gospel of eternal salvation to the world. I solemnly promised Him that I would dedicate my entire life to His active service.

At that time I was living with my parents in Florida. My mother's prayer was for me to preach the Gospel, but my father did not want me to be a minister.

Early one morning as my father was eating breakfast in the dining room, I explained to him that I had definitely decided to preach. I told him that I was leaving home that day to accompany a young evangelist and that, first, we were going to conduct a revival meeting in a rural school building.

My Irish father roughly warned me that, generally, ministers lack the comforts of life. Then he reminded me of the money he had already spent on me to follow another profession. He said that, no doubt, I would starve if I went out to preach and that I could expect no help from him.

As he walked out the door to go to work, he pointed a finger at me and said he expected to find me at home when he returned.

My Battle With Fear

To say I was brokenhearted would be too mild: I was crushed. Besides bringing me sorrow, my father's unbending attitude struck terror in my heart. His words, *You will starve!* kept booming in my mind and heart. A seventeen-year-old thinks his dad is a fair authority on most subjects, especially on how to get along in life. My father's words caused the darkness of hell to cover my life.

I could not obey both my heavenly Father and my earthly father. I staggered back to my bedroom, trembling at the thought of disobeying either one. Weeping bitterly, I fell to my knees beside my bed and began praying desperately to Christ. Then I heard a voice within me. It was the Inner Voice of Divine Guidance, which I have come to know intimately through the years. The Voice told me to read Isaiah 41:10,11. Unfamiliar at that time with the passage, I turned to it and read aloud:

Fear thou not; for I am with thee: be not dismayed; for I am thy God: I will strengthen thee; yea, I will help thee; yea, I will uphold thee with the right hand of my righteousness.

Behold, all they that were incensed against thee shall be ashamed and confounded: they shall be as nothing; and they that strive with thee shall perish.

The Bible Makes a Man

Possibly that moment is too sacred to describe. The blending of the human and divine in that spiritually illuminating and holy invigorating meeting is impossible to express. As I realized how definitely, positively, and lovingly Omnipotence was speaking to me—to *me,* an inexperienced youth—I was humbled.

Each phrase of that Scripture passage spoke dynamically to my personal situation as if it had been written just for me!

Fear thou not! This direct command from my God had the greatest effect of all the phrases upon my mind and spirit. Like a cloud lifting, fear dispelled from my heart instantly. Fear of the future, fear of failure, fear of hunger—all were gone! Suddenly within my breast, the music of triumph was sounding a victory march! God had performed a miracle—a boy's heart had been made into a man's heart.

The second clause of this scripture gave the reason for the first: *Fear thou not; for **I am with thee.*** As I gazed at those words through the prism of my tears, they became a fortress of strength.

I thought, *Mother's God is going with me to preach! My pastor's Lord is going with me to battle! The Jehovah Who had performed the miracles of the Bible—the God of Moses, Joshua, David, and Daniel—is going along with me as a companion!*

I laughed and I wept. I stood up, looked out over the lovely blue waters of St. Andrew's Bay, then knelt again by the bed. I had been transported into a new world. I felt ready to run through a troop and jump over a wall. (Ps. 18:29.)

Looking at the scripture again, I read the third clause: *Be not dismayed.* The word *dismay* means "loss of courage; horrified amazement; being reduced to despair."

My condition at that moment fit the description. Fear had made me lose my courage for God and had left me in a state of horrified amazement. But God marvelously drove despair from my life. He revealed to me that as His servant I would not know permanent defeat or despair.

The fourth clause contained the positive Source of deliverance: . . . *for I am thy God.* The Living God. Not an idol of stone or gold, not a god with ears that cannot hear and eyes that cannot see, but a present help in time of trouble. (Ps. 46:1.) How thrilling it was for me, a young man, to hear God speak with such assurances!

I read the fifth clause: *I will strengthen thee.* It is hard for others to imagine what those words meant to a youth, having been so recently raised up from a bed of tuberculosis. The battle ahead would be long and hard. I needed divine strength, and I could feel it flowing into every fiber of my being as I knelt in God's presence.

In the sixth clause God continued: *Yea, I will help thee.* God was doubly emphasizing, assuring, and promising that in *every* emergency He would be there to assist me and to give me strength.

The seventh clause affirmed: *Yea, I will uphold thee with the right hand of my righteousness.* This "right hand" speaks of God's power, His authority. The assurance that God would be upholding me with His right hand was the greatest security I could have received.

Any minister who goes forth without the above group of promises in his briefcase will never be able to preach the Gospel!

I understood how to minister after reading verse 10. From verse 11, I learned how to take care of some personal problems:

Behold, all they that were incensed against thee shall be ashamed and confounded: they shall be as nothing; and they that strive with thee shall perish. This was to be my armor. I did not need to fight my own battles—God would fight them for me!

When I had finished studying this passage, my heart was filled with love, joy, and faith. Fear was gone. Dismay was defeated. Weakness was past. God had undergirded my spiritual life.

Immediately, I packed my suitcase and left my father's house.

From that hour, God has helped me to bring deliverance to thousands of people who are bound by fear. If any special gift of God is present in my life, it is to assist and lift from depression those who are afflicted by fear phobias.

Remember, *God is no respecter of persons* (Acts 10:34). His Word is of no private interpretation. (2 Pet. 1:20.) God can make Isaiah 41:10,11 meet *your* personal needs just like He made it meet mine.

7

The Battle Cry
Seven Steps to Victory

For God hath not given us the spirit of fear; but of power, and of love, and of a sound mind.

2 Timothy 1:7

In the past chapters we pulled the ugly mask off our deadly enemy, fear. We learned how fear originated and that its originator was the Devil. We saw the ways fear attacks the human personality. Through prophecy we saw how fear will increase in the last days. But then we learned that the mind of Christ will be our strength in those terrible times.

In this last chapter we will study how people terrorized by this Black Monster can meet, defeat, and destroy its tormenting phobias.

When Fear Strikes

When fear strikes, take the following seven steps:

1. Recognize it.
2. Analyze it.
3. Externalize it.
4. Resist it with action.
5. Fight it with the Bible.
6. Fight it with prayer.
7. Consult a minister.

1. Recognize Fear

Many sick people refuse to accept the fact that they have a disease. Life to them becomes a game of hide and seek. Saying that something doesn't exist *never* makes it disappear.

If you have a fear phobia, say so! Part of the victory comes with recognizing a problem situation. Once you have recognized it, then you can become alert to possible solutions.

The most dangerous kind of enemy is a hidden one. Often, fears lay hidden in the subconscious mind. Until you recognize them by bringing them into your conscious mind, you will never know how to combat the enemy.

Do not blame your symptoms on some other person or on conditions beyond your control: failing economic conditions, world political troubles, unfriendly home or office situations. These cannot fill you with fear without your mental permission.

Do not hide from fear. To see the way out of your troubles, you must meet fear ''open souled.''

Do not try to dismiss fear as the fruit of superstition. If that were the case, many cultured, highly talented, well-educated people would never be afflicted. But they are. Of those consulting me, some of the people most seriously afflicted with fear were highly educated. One man, a doctor of philosophy, lived a frightened life behind closed doors. Fear had driven him from his responsibilities as a university instructor.

The power of positive prayer offered by a number of his friends delivered him and returned him to successful work again. The last time I saw him, he was radiantly successful and abundantly blessed by God.

Some people feel that recognizing fears is cowardly. But remember the well-known adage: Cowards die a thousand deaths; the courageous taste death but once.

When fear creeps into dangerous situations, you must do your best to overcome it. To run or quit is cowardice, and nobody applauds a coward. You must go boldly to battle against fear. There is no other way to victory. At times, a habitual loser can become animated with a spirit that creates a winner. I saw this once years ago in a very interesting primitive battle between a little rat and a big snake.

While doing missionary evangelism in the deep jungles of South America, I spent time at an Anglican mission station. As I was standing with the local missionary, talking, we witnessed an amazing sight, more amazing than anything I had ever seen.

We saw a large snake coming out of the barn, moving in a fast and unusual way. Before I could ask my friend what was wrong with the snake, a large rat came from the barn in full pursuit. The rat plunged at the snake and bit it, causing it to jerk forward. Then it jumped at the snake and bit it again.

The snake was obviously in pain. Rather than stopping for combat, the snake moved away as quickly as possible, only to be bitten again. It was one of the most amusing battles I had ever seen: a ten-foot serpent running from a ten-inch rat!

The missionary explained that usually the snake would be the master and kill the rat; but in this instance, the snake enraged the rat by accidently disturbing her nest. The mother, instinctively propelled to preserve her young, viciously attacked the snake. Her savage attack so caught him off guard that it compelled him to retreat! The weak attacked and defeated the strong!

In this incident I saw how having objectives and determination in life give fighting power over fear. The spirit of battle has much to do with who wins. You can feel weaker than your adversary, yet still gain a great victory because of the spirit to win.

2. Analyze Fear

Fears have real causes. Just as the bite of a mosquito is the cause of malaria, so is a real incident the cause of fear.

When you feel fear coming on you, analyze the situation. Search back into your life to see if you are running from something you should face. Try to remember the very first time you were terribly afraid, and what caused it. Determine how many times you have been frantically afraid, and what happened just before fear struck you.

Ask some close friends or members of the family if they are afraid of the same thing. If not, why not?

In a dangerous situation, all people involved will be afraid together. When a hurricane blows full blast upon a city, toppling houses right and left, the people of the city are equally afraid because the danger is real. If a lion escapes his cage and roams down Main Street, all people who encounter the lion will be afraid for the situation is truly dangerous.

If others are not afraid of something with you, your fears are unreal. Take this as an indication that you need assistance to rid yourself of a phobia which, if not dealt with, could wreck your life.

3. Externalize Fear

Force fear into your conscious mind, into your rational world. Don't repress fear, sending it back into your subconscious mind. Externalize your fears.

When I was in Alaska conducting revival meetings, I stayed in the home of the pastor. One afternoon I took his five-year-old daughter for a walk, not knowing that she had a horror of dogs.

As we walked along the sidewalk, a large dog lumbered toward us, wagging his tail and licking the fingers of anyone who would stop to pat him. When he started toward the little girl, she screamed and grabbed me in terror, her face pale with fear. The dog, paying no attention, ran on down the street.

We walked on. I told the child that the dog especially liked little girls and would not harm her, and that dogs have saved the lives of little girls sometimes.

Within five minutes we saw another dog as large and friendly as the first. He came to us and thrust his nose at her. She reached a trembling hand toward him and mumbled, "You are a nice doggy, aren't you? You like little girls!" He wagged his tail, then meandered off. Laughing and skipping, the little girl said, "Dogs are nice to little girls, aren't they?" "They surely are," I assured her.

She had won a wonderful victory by replacing fear with faith. Once she brought her fears into the open and saw that they were not founded on fact, she used her faith to destroy them.

4. Resist Fear with Action

Many people are easily overwhelmed by fear and take refuge behind closed doors. According to Benjamin Franklin, ''God helps those who help themselves.'' You must fight fear with all your physical, moral, and spiritual strength. Never yield to a fear phobia or give up hope of victory. You must have the spirit to fight back against your fears. Until you are willing to actively resist fear, no one can help you.

Better hospitals and a greater number of better-trained psychiatrists will not solve the fear problem. We must show the people that God will arm them to resist fear and empty those hospitals already occupied beyond capacity!

Once, when I was preaching among the tribes of Mexico, a Mexican friend told me of an interesting occurrence.

In Yucatan, where the Mayan Indians live, there is an ancient well which, according to legend, was used for sacrifice. Whenever a drought, flood, plague, or terrible storm approached, the tribal leaders chose a young virgin from one of the leading families of the tribe and sacrificed her to appease the anger of the gods.

The ceremony involved cutting out the virgin's heart and offering it to the fierce gods, then burying the virgin in the sacred well. A precious object was always buried with the virgin. Many virgins and many treasures were at the bottom of the well.

According to Indian tradition, if any person disturbed the well by touching the sacred waters, he would die instantly and bring the gods' anger upon the entire tribe. Fear kept the local Indians from seeking the treasures.

A visitor to the area heard the story from the travel guides. Upon inquiring of the old men of the tribe, he found that because no one had ever searched the well for fear of death, no one knew whether or not the story was true.

The visitor did not believe he would die and refused to be afraid. One night, alone, he descended by a ladder into the depths of the well. Using steel hooks to fish in the "magic" waters, he found among the bones ancient treasures. The man informed his guide that the legend of the bones and treasures at the bottom of the well was true. He left the next day with boxes of articles that no one in the community ever saw.

That man broke the spell of fear over the natives. They realized, though too late, that superstition had kept them from the treasures.

Fear and superstition can keep *you* from the best things in life. By resisting fear actively, you will win a great victory.

5. Fight Fear with the Bible

The only living book in existence is the Bible. Because the Bible is a divine revelation, it possesses supernatural power.

The Apostle Paul tells us in Hebrews 4:12 that God's Word is a sword with power to divide the spirit and the mind. Since the mind is the center from which come fears, the Bible is the greatest instrument in destroying fear.

The Apostle Paul further stated, *Faith cometh by hearing, and hearing by the word of God* (Rom. 10:17). This means the very power to resist fear is derived from God's Word entering into our being. It is very important that you read the Bible aloud and hear it read in your church.

The phrases, *fear not* and *be not afraid,* appear at least 100 times in the Bible.

God spoke to Abraham and said, *Fear not* (Gen. 15:1).

God spoke to the children of Israel and said, *Fear ye not, stand still, and see the salvation of the Lord* (Ex. 14:13).

The great patriarch David said, *Though I walk through the valley of the shadow of death, I will fear no evil* (Ps. 23:4).

Here are just twelve of the precious promises you can use in gaining victory over fear:

1. *For God hath not given us the spirit of fear; but of power, and of love, and of a sound mind* (2 Tim. 1:7).

2. *Ye shall not be afraid of the face of man; for the judgment is God's* (Deut. 1:17).

3. *Fear not, nor be dismayed, be strong and of good courage* (Josh. 10:25).

4. *I will trust, and not be afraid: for the Lord Jehovah is my strength and my song* (Is. 12:2).

5. *O man greatly beloved, fear not: peace be unto thee, be strong, yea, be strong* (Dan. 10:19).

6. *For he shall give his angels charge over thee, to keep thee in all thy ways* (Ps. 91:11).

7. *God is our refuge and strength, a very present help in trouble. Therefore will not we fear* (Ps. 46:1,2).

8. *I will never leave thee, nor forsake thee* (Heb. 13:5).

9. *The Lord is my helper, and I will not fear what man shall do unto me* (Heb. 13:6).

10. *Fear ye not therefore, ye are of more value than many sparrows* (Matt. 10:31).

11. *Thou wilt keep him in perfect peace, whose mind is stayed on thee: because he trusteth in thee* (Is. 26:3).

12. *Fear ye not the reproach of men, neither be ye afraid of their revilings* (Is. 51:7).

6. Fight Fear with Prayer

True prayer is not a mystic practice, nor is it merely an emotional experience. Christian prayer is not the voice of a weakling who is begging for assistance. By *prayer*, I do not mean reading prayers from a book or quoting a prayer from memory. When I speak of prayer, I am referring to a heart-to-heart talk with God.

There is power in prayer. Praying generates spiritual strength and assurance. Dr. Alexis S. Carroll once said, ''Prayer, our deepest source of power and perfection, has been left miserably underdeveloped.'' This scientifically minded physician reveals a great truth. If people of our land used this deepest source of power, they would not be terrorized by fear.

Prayer is like a compass. As ships and planes are guided by a compass in natural life, every person is guided by prayer in spiritual life. The less you pray, the less you know about how to live.

The great writer, Ralph Waldo Emerson, said, "No man ever prayed without learning something." Prayer is not futile talking. The words prayed to the Infinite Source of energy strengthen humans' finite power. By addressing God in prayer, you link your life with the power that moves the universe.

The great men of the Bible performed their heroic feats by prayer. When Elijah (called Elias in the New Testament) prayed, God answered by sending rain. (James 5:17,18.) When Christ prayed, wonderful miracles took place. Now *you* must pray. Your prayers can repel, expel, and dispel fear.

Singing also brings victory over fear. The grand inspirational hymn,

"Leaning on the Everlasting Arms," is a sample of this:

> *What have I to dread,*
> *What have I to fear,*
> *Leaning on the everlasting arms?*
>
> *I have blessed peace*
> *With my Lord so near,*
> *Leaning on the everlasting arms.*

Prayer and praise will sustain you with the security of everlasting arms.

7. Consult a Minister

One of the best ways to rid yourself of fear is to have a heart-to-heart talk with a sympathetic and intelligent person. I recommend that you consult a minister of the Gospel.

The minister, whether an evangelist or a pastor, is a man set apart by God. He deals every day with problems of the soul, mind, and spirit, and is acquainted with your type of need.

If you do not attend church, I suggest that you do so very soon. Get acquainted with the minister. Ask him for an appointment to help you deal with a personal problem. He will be ready and happy to serve you. Follow his instructions carefully.

When you have honestly done your part to destroy fear, God will work with you to do the rest!

The Bliss To Come

It would be wonderful to awaken one morning and discover that no one had any fears: that there was nothing to be afraid of; that there were no more fears of insanity, disease, job loss, fire, or any other calamity; that no one in the world feared secret police bursting in to take him to prison.

It would be wonderful to awaken and find that everybody everywhere possessed a deep, vibrant joy!

That day **will** come! John the Beloved was able to see it. He recorded it in The Revelation, the final book of the Bible:

And I saw a new heaven and a new earth . . . And God shall wipe away all tears from their eyes; and there shall be no more death, neither sorrow, nor crying, neither shall there be any more pain: for the former things are passed away (Rev. 21:1,4).

And there shall be no more curse . . . And there shall be no night there (Rev. 22:3,5).

And there shall be no more fear!

The Christian life is the best one on Earth and the only one in the world to come!

If you have not made your decision to accept Christ as Savior, do it *now . . .*

If thou shalt confess with thy mouth the Lord Jesus, and shalt believe in thine heart that God hath raised him from the dead, thou shalt be saved.

For with the heart man believeth unto righteousness; and with the mouth confession is made unto salvation.

Romans 10:9,10

MY CHALLENGE TO YOU

If Jesus should come today, would you be ready? If you are not sure, I invite you to receive Jesus as your Savior now. You will be filled with hope and peace that only Jesus can offer.

Pray out loud with me right now:

"Dear Lord Jesus, I am a sinner. I do believe that you died and rose from the dead to save me from my sins. I want to be with you in heaven forever. God, forgive me of all my sins that I have committed against you. I here and now open my heart to you and ask you to come into my heart and life and be my personal Savior. Amen."

When you pray the Sinner's Prayer and mean it, He will come in instantly. You are now a child of God and you have been transferred from the devil's dominion to the kingdom of God. Read I John 1:9 and Colossians 1:13. A wonderful peace and joy will fill your soul.

Please write and tell me what Jesus has done for you. I will send you a little pamphlet titled, "So You're Born Again!" Mail your letter to: **Lester Sumrall, P.O. Box 12, South Bend, IN 46624.**

ABOUT OUR MINISTRY

The Lester Sumrall Evangelical Association ... LESEA, INC. Founded in 1957 by Lester Sumrall, LESEA is a multi-faceted ministry with a vision to proclaim the uncompromised Gospel message of Jesus Christ to the World.

Today, the ministry of LESEA continues to touch all four corners of the globe. Through television, radio, the printed page, education facilities, and an international relief organization, LESEA meets the needs of people mentally, physically and most of all, spiritually.

"For we are not ashamed of the gospel of Christ: for it is the power of God unto salvation to everyone who believes..."
Romans 1:16

LESEA GLOBAL FEED THE HUNGRY

LESEA Global Feed The Hungry was created in 1987 to feed hungry people around the world and provide emergency relief to those in need as the result of famine, drought, flood, war, or other disasters.

Our Vision is simple...bring the abundance of God's people in the first world to meet the need of God's people in the third world, strengthening the church and evangelizing the lost in the process. We are a pastor to pastor, church to church program responding to the biblical mandate to feed the hungry.

Our ocean-going sea worthy vessel, the M.V. Evangeline, provides cost efficient and timely aid. Owning and operating a ship with the ability to deliver 4 thousand tons of cargo in a single drop gives LESEA Global Feed The Hungry a unique approach as we successfully answer the challenges of this present age. LESEA Global Feed The

Hungry can respond immediately to disaster situations around the world with more than 65 volunteer directors with representation in 20 nations. With one telephone call, we can start the wheels rolling to help relieve those caught in desperate situations.

LESEA BROADCASTING

In 1967, LESEA set the stage for a worldwide broadcasting division with the construction of radio station WHME-FM in South Bend, Indiana. The LESEA Broadcasting network now includes a variety of radio and television stations, a fulltime satellite channel and a number of shortwave radio stations. Potentially, 100% of the world can see or hear one of LESEA's broadcasts.

Television and radio are probably the most persuasive mediums of communication in existence. They have had more impact on our society and its culture, moral and ethical values than any other vehicles known to man.

It is LESEA's belief that television, radio and shortwave should uplift, educate and inspire people to strive for a better life.

LESEA TOURS

LESEA Tours is a full-service travel agency capable of meeting all types of travel needs by land, air, or sea. For over 30 years, LESEA Tours has organized pilgrimmages to Israel, providing special services and memorable experiences for thousands of Holy Land travelers.

LESEA WORLD HARVEST PRAYLINE

Realizing people's need for direction and encouragement could happen at any time of the day or night, LESEA established "Prayerline." Dedicated, trained volunteers man the phones 24-hours a day, and are ready to pray and encourage people during their times of need. LESEA's Prayline can reached at (219) 291-1010, or via the Internet at www.worldharvest.com

BOOKS BY DR. LESTER SUMRALL

- Adventuring With Christ
- My Story To His Glory
- Take It–It's Yours
- Gifts & Ministries Of The Holy Spirit
- Alien Entities
- Battle Of The Ages
- Conscience–The Scales Of Eternal Justice
- Demons The Answer Book
- Bitten By Devils
- Ecstasy–Finding Joy In Living
- Faith To Change The World
- Faith Under Siege; The Life of Abraham
- Faith-Filled Words (Frank Sumrall)
- Fishers Of Men
- Gates Of Hell
- Genesis–Crucible Of The Universe
- Hostility
- Hypnotism–Divine Or Demonic
- Imagination–Hidden Force Of Human Potential
- Jerusalem,   Where Empires Die–
           Will America Die At Jerusalem?
- Living Free
- Making Life Count
- Miracles Don't Just Happen
- 101 Questions & Answers On Demon Power
- Paul–Man Of The Millennia
- Run With The Vision
- Secrets Of Answered Prayer
- Sixty Things God Said About Sex
- Supernatural Principalities & Powers
- The Making Of A Champion
- The Names Of God
- The Promises Of God
- The Reality Of Angels
- The Stigma Of Calvary
- The Total Man
- Trajectory Of Faith–Joseph
- Three Habitations Of Devels
- Unprovoked Murder
- Victory And Dominion Over Fear
- You Can Conquer GRIEF Before It Conquers You

Sumrall Publishing Company, Inc.
P.O. Box 12, South Bend, Indiana 46624